Inventory Management

by Dwayne Farr

———————

Introduction to Inventory Management

Extended Version:

Inventory management plays a critical role in the success of any business that deals with physical goods. It involves the careful control and monitoring of inventory levels to ensure a smooth and efficient supply chain. This chapter will delve deeper into the different facets of inventory management, providing a comprehensive understanding of the subject.

One key component of effective inventory management is the implementation of inventory control systems. These systems employ various methods to keep track of inventory levels, monitor stock movements, and facilitate timely replenishment. Some commonly used inventory control systems include periodic review systems, perpetual inventory systems, and Just-in-Time (JIT) systems.

Periodic review systems involve conducting periodic physical counts of inventory and placing orders to replenish stock at predetermined intervals. This system requires maintaining safety stock levels to buffer against demand variability. On the other hand, perpetual inventory systems rely on continuous monitoring of inventory levels through the use of technology like barcode scanning or radio frequency identification (RFID). These systems provide real-time data on inventory levels, helping businesses make informed decisions about reordering and managing stock.

JIT systems focus on minimizing inventory levels by synchronizing the arrival of goods with their demand. This lean approach aims to reduce storage costs, minimize the risk of obsolescence, and improve operational efficiency. By closely collaborating with suppliers and adopting efficient production strategies, businesses implementing JIT can create a streamlined supply chain that minimizes inventory holding costs.

Demand forecasting is crucial for inventory management as it helps businesses anticipate future demand patterns and plan their stock accordingly. Numerous forecasting techniques, such as trend analysis, moving averages, and predictive analytics, can be employed to predict demand based on historical data, market trends, and external factors. Accurate demand forecasting enables businesses to maintain optimal inventory levels, avoid stockouts, minimize excess inventory, and optimize order quantities. Advanced forecasting tools and software can provide businesses with greater accuracy and enhance decision-making capabilities.

Another key concept in inventory management is the application of lean principles. Lean aims to eliminate waste, increase efficiency, and optimize processes. In the context of inventory, lean principles can be applied to reduce excess inventory, eliminate stockouts, and improve overall supply chain performance. One example of using lean principles is the implementation of Kanban systems, which enable just-in-time inventory replenishment by visually signaling when inventory needs to be restocked. By visualizing the flow of materials and aligning production with actual demand, businesses can reduce waste, optimize order quantities, and improve overall efficiency.

Supplier relationship management is another critical aspect of inventory management. Building strong relationships with suppliers helps businesses ensure a reliable and timely supply of goods. Regular communication, accurate demand forecasts, clear expectations, and mutually beneficial relationships contribute to improved inventory management. Collaboration with suppliers on issues like lead times, transportation costs, and order frequency can result in cost savings, leaner inventory levels, and improved customer service.

Warehouse organization and layout optimization are instrumental in efficient inventory management. Well-organized warehouses and inventory systems reduce picking errors, improve order fulfillment speed, and enhance the overall accuracy of inventory data. Employing techniques like ABC analysis, which categorizes items based on their importance, can assist in prioritizing inventory control efforts and identifying slow-moving or obsolete items.

Accurate inventory counts are critical for inventory management. Regular stock audits and implementation of technologies like barcode scanning or RFID tagging ensure that inventory levels are reliable and up to date. By reducing discrepancies and maintaining accurate inventory data, businesses can make informed decisions about reorder points, safety stock levels, and replenishment strategies.

Replenishment strategies play a significant role in efficient inventory management. Businesses need to determine optimal order quantities, reorder points, and lead times to ensure continuous stock availability while avoiding overstocking. Traditional methods like Economic Order Quantity (EOQ) and reorder point analysis aid in optimizing replenishment decisions. EOQ calculates the order quantity that minimizes the total cost of ordering and holding inventory. Reorder point analysis determines the inventory level at which a new order should be placed to prevent stockouts.

To measure the effectiveness of inventory management efforts, businesses should establish key performance metrics. Metrics like inventory turnover ratio, stockout rate, order fulfillment speed, and carrying costs provide valuable insights into inventory performance. Regular monitoring of these metrics helps identify areas for improvement, assess the impact of inventory management strategies, and evaluate the overall efficiency of the inventory management system.

In conclusion, effective inventory management is crucial for the success of any business that deals with physical goods. By implementing appropriate inventory control systems, incorporating demand forecasting techniques, applying lean principles, fostering strong supplier relationships, optimizing warehouse organization, ensuring inventory accuracy, adopting replenishment strategies, and measuring performance metrics, businesses can achieve optimal stock levels, minimize costs, improve customer satisfaction, and enhance operational efficiency. With the right strategies and tools, businesses can master the art of inventory management and gain a competitive edge in their industry.

Understanding Inventory Control Systems

Inventory control systems play a vital role in managing inventory effectively for businesses across diverse industries. These systems encompass a range of methodologies and tools that enable businesses to monitor and control the flow of goods throughout their supply chain. By implementing the right inventory control system, businesses can optimize inventory levels, minimize costs, improve customer satisfaction, and enhance overall operational efficiency.

To gain a comprehensive understanding of inventory control systems, it is essential to delve deeper into the intricacies of each type. Let's explore the different types of inventory control systems in greater detail:

1. Manual Inventory Control Systems: Manual inventory control systems are traditional methods of managing inventory through manual recording using spreadsheets or paper-based tracking systems. While seemingly outdated in a digitalized world, they are still employed in some business settings. These systems require manual data entry for tracking inventory-related activities such as stock receipts, adjustments, and sales. Although simple and cost-effective, manual systems are more prone to human errors, can be time-consuming, and lack real-time visibility into inventory levels.

2. Perpetual Inventory Control Systems: Perpetual inventory control systems leverage technologies like barcode scanning or radio-frequency identification (RFID) to provide real-time updates on inventory levels. These systems automatically track inventory movement as goods are received, stored, or sold. Each item in the inventory is assigned a unique identifier linked to a database that stores pertinent details such as item description, quantity, location, and transaction history. With perpetual inventory control, businesses have accurate and up-to-date information, allowing for effective decision making related to inventory replenishment, order fulfillment, and demand forecasting.

3. Just-in-Time (JIT) Inventory Control Systems: Just-in-Time inventory control systems aim to optimize inventory levels by synchronizing production and supply with customer demand.

In JIT systems, inventory is acquired and produced precisely when it is needed, minimizing excess stock. This approach requires close coordination between suppliers and businesses to ensure materials and products are delivered promptly. By reducing the carrying costs associated with excess inventory, JIT systems improve cash flow and minimize storage space requirements. However, JIT systems necessitate highly efficient supply chains, effective demand forecasting, and continuous communication to mitigate the risks associated with unexpected demand fluctuations or disruptions in the supply chain.

4. Batch Control Inventory Systems: Industries dealing with perishables or specific production cycles often employ batch control systems. In these systems, inventory is treated as batches or lots, and each batch is assigned a unique identifier. Batch control systems enable better management of expiration dates, facilitate product recall traceability, and aid in quality control. For example, in the pharmaceutical industry, batch control systems ensure adherence to strict regulations and enable the tracking of specific batches throughout the distribution process. Additionally, these systems provide valuable insights into product quality, allowing businesses to take appropriate actions if issues arise.

5. Automated Inventory Control Systems: Automated inventory control systems utilize advanced technologies like artificial intelligence (AI), machine learning (ML), and cloud computing to streamline inventory management processes. These systems automate various tasks, including inventory tracking, demand forecasting, order management, and replenishment. By analyzing historical data, market trends, and customer trends, automated systems can provide valuable insights to optimize inventory levels, minimize stockouts, and reduce carrying costs. AI and ML algorithms can learn from historical data patterns and adapt to dynamic market conditions, enabling businesses to make data-driven decisions to enhance operational efficiency.

When selecting an inventory control system, businesses need to carefully evaluate their specific inventory management requirements. Factors such as industry, business size, complexity, financial capabilities, and technological infrastructure should be considered. Implementing an appropriate inventory control system allows businesses to enhance efficiency, reduce costs, improve customer satisfaction, and gain a competitive edge in their respective markets.

The Role of Technology in Inventory Management

In today's fast-paced business environment, technology plays a crucial and ever-evolving role in effectively managing inventory. With the advancements in digital tools, automation, and data analytics, businesses can streamline their inventory processes, improve accuracy, optimize stock levels, and enhance overall efficiency. This chapter explores in-depth the various ways in which technology can revolutionize inventory management.

1. Inventory Tracking Systems: Technology has revolutionized inventory tracking systems, significantly improving the accuracy and efficiency of tracking and monitoring inventory levels. Traditional manual methods, such as pen and paper or spreadsheets, were time-consuming, prone to errors, and lacked real-time visibility. However, with the advent of barcode scanning systems and inventory management software, businesses can now automate inventory tracking and have real-time information on stock levels, locations, and movement.

Barcode scanning systems use barcode labels or tags that can be quickly scanned using handheld devices or fixed scanners. This technology eliminates manual data entry errors, speeds up the process of receiving and picking items, and enhances inventory accuracy. Inventory management software, on the other hand, provides a centralized platform for organizing and tracking inventory, automatically updating stock levels as sales occur, and generating real-time reports and alerts when replenishment is required. By utilizing technologies such as RFID (Radio-frequency Identification) tags and sensors, businesses can achieve seamless and accurate tracking throughout the supply chain, reducing stock discrepancies, preventing theft, and improving overall logistics operations.

2. Demand Forecasting and Planning: Technology has greatly enhanced the capabilities of forecasting and demand planning in inventory management. Advanced algorithms and data analytics tools can analyze vast amounts of historical sales data, market trends, customer behavior, and external factors to accurately predict future demand patterns.

Demand forecasting and planning software utilizes sophisticated statistical models, machine learning algorithms, and artificial intelligence to extract meaningful insights from large datasets. These tools can identify seasonality, trends, and patterns, allowing businesses to make informed decisions regarding inventory levels, procurement, production scheduling, and promotions. By leveraging these technologies, businesses can optimize their inventory levels, reduce stockouts and excess inventory, align production and procurement with demand, and minimize the risk of obsolete stock. This results in improved customer satisfaction, reduced holding costs, and increased profitability.

3. Automated Reordering Systems: Maintaining optimal inventory levels can be a complex and challenging task for businesses. Technology has simplified this process through the introduction of automated reordering systems. By setting up reorder points, safety stock levels, lead times, and integrating them with real-time sales data, businesses can automate the replenishment process.

Automated reordering systems continuously monitor inventory levels and trigger replenishment actions when stock levels fall below predetermined thresholds. This eliminates the need for manual intervention and reduces the risk of stockouts or excess inventory. Advanced algorithms can even consider factors such as seasonality and market trends to optimize the reorder points and quantities automatically. Additionally, some sophisticated systems can integrate with suppliers' systems, allowing them to directly receive signals to initiate the replenishment process. This streamlines the entire supply chain, reduces lead times, and increases operational efficiency.

4. Warehouse Management Systems: Efficient warehouse operations are crucial for effective inventory management. Technology has played a significant role in optimizing warehouse processes through the adoption of Warehouse Management Systems (WMS).

WMS software helps businesses better organize their inventory, optimize space utilization, improve picking accuracy, and reduce fulfillment cycle times. These systems provide functionalities such as automated pick lists, barcode scanning, real-time inventory updates, and location tracking, enabling businesses to achieve higher productivity, lower costs, and improved customer satisfaction.

Advanced WMS solutions also offer features such as wave planning, which optimizes the picking process by grouping orders with common characteristics to minimize travel distances and maximize efficiency. Cross-docking capabilities allow for the direct transfer of goods from receiving to outbound shipping, reducing the need for storage and handling. Furthermore, innovations such as robotics, automated guided vehicles (AGVs), and artificial intelligence (AI) are revolutionizing warehouse operations further, facilitating faster and error-free picking, packing, and shipping processes.

5. Integration with Supply Chain Partners: Technology has enabled seamless integration and

information sharing between different entities in the supply chain. Through Electronic Data Interchange (EDI), Application Programming Interfaces (APIs), and cloud-based platforms, businesses can collaborate with suppliers, vendors, and logistics partners in real-time.

Integration with suppliers allows for the automation of processes such as order placement, confirmation, and tracking. By electronically sharing real-time sales data, businesses enable suppliers to proactively manage inventory levels and replenish stock when needed, reducing stockouts and improving supply chain efficiency. This integration also facilitates efficient order processing, improved visibility, and faster lead times.

Similarly, integration with logistics partners allows for real-time tracking of shipments, enhancing transparency and on-time delivery. By sharing shipment information, businesses can accurately estimate arrival times, optimize inventory positioning, and quickly resolve any delivery issues. This level of visibility and collaboration throughout the supply chain promotes strategic decision-making, reduces costs, and enhances customer satisfaction.

6. Internet of Things (IoT) and Advanced Analytics: The Internet of Things (IoT) and advanced analytics are driving major advancements in inventory management. IoT sensors embedded in products, containers, or shelves can provide real-time data on location, temperature, humidity, and even product usage. This data, when combined with advanced analytics, enables businesses to gain deeper insights into their inventory performance.

IoT sensors capture information from various touchpoints within the supply chain and transmit it to a centralized system for analysis. Advanced analytics tools can process this data in real-time, identify trends and anomalies, and generate actionable insights. For example, businesses can monitor the condition of perishable goods during transportation and storage, ensuring compliance with quality standards and reducing waste. They can also analyze historical inventory data to identify slow-moving or obsolete items and adjust their purchasing and pricing strategies accordingly. By leveraging this technology, businesses can make data-driven decisions, improve forecasting accuracy, reduce waste, and proactively manage their inventory.

7. Blockchain Technology: Blockchain technology is gaining traction in inventory management due to its potential to enhance transparency, traceability, and trust in supply chains.

Blockchain, a decentralized and secure ledger system, allows multiple parties to have access to a shared source of truth without the need for intermediaries. By recording all transactions and movements of goods on the blockchain, businesses can eliminate disputes, reduce counterfeiting, and ensure the authenticity of products. This technology is particularly beneficial for industries such as pharmaceuticals, luxury goods, and food supply chains, where traceability and quality control are vital.

For pharmaceutical supply chains, blockchain can enable the tracking of drugs from the manufacturer to the end consumer, minimizing the risk of counterfeit or substandard products entering the market. In the luxury goods industry, blockchain can provide proof of authenticity and ownership, reducing the prevalence of counterfeit items. In food supply chains, blockchain can enable complete traceability, allowing consumers to verify the origin, safety, and quality of the products they purchase.

In conclusion, technology continues to transform inventory management practices, enabling businesses to gain better control over their inventory, improve accuracy, optimize stock levels, reduce costs, and enhance customer satisfaction. Adopting the right technology solutions and staying updated with the latest trends in inventory management can provide businesses with a competitive edge in today's dynamic marketplace. As technology evolves further, integrating emerging technologies like AI, robotics, blockchain, and predictive analytics will continue to push the boundariesof what is possible in inventory management. The ongoing advancements in technology will continue to shape the future of inventory management and present new opportunities for businesses to further optimize their operations.

One area that holds immense potential is the integration of artificial intelligence (AI) and machine learning (ML) in inventory management systems. AI-powered inventory management algorithms can analyze vast amounts of data, quickly identify patterns, and make intelligent predictions. For example, AI algorithms can analyze historical sales data, customer behavior, market trends, and even external factors like weather patterns to accurately forecast demand and optimize inventory levels.

ML algorithms can continuously learn and improve over time, adapting to changing market conditions and refining demand forecasts. These AI-powered systems can automatically adjust reorder points, safety stock levels, and lead times to optimize inventory management, reducing stockouts and excess inventory.

In addition to AI and ML, robotics and automation are transforming the warehouse and fulfillment processes. Automated picking and packing systems can significantly increase efficiency while reducing errors. Robots can handle repetitive and labor-intensive tasks, allowing human workers to focus on more complex and value-added activities. Advanced robotic systems, such as autonomous mobile robots (AMRs) and robotic arms, can navigate warehouses and pick items with speed and accuracy.

Furthermore, the integration of inventory management systems with e-commerce platforms and omnichannel retail strategies is becoming increasingly important. With the rise of online shopping and the growing customer demand for seamless shopping experiences across various channels, businesses need to ensure inventory accuracy and visibility across their entire sales ecosystem. Integrating inventory management systems with e-commerce platforms allows for real-time inventory updates, accurate order fulfillment, and efficient stock allocation across physical stores, warehouses, and online channels.

Cloud-based inventory management solutions are also gaining popularity due to their scalability, flexibility, and accessibility. Cloud-based systems enable businesses to store and access inventory data in a centralized platform, accessible from anywhere and at any time. This eliminates the need for physical servers and infrastructure, reducing costs and providing real-time access to inventory information for all stakeholders.

As businesses navigate an increasingly globalized and complex supply chain landscape, technology can help mitigate risks and increase efficiency. Supply chain visibility platforms and track-and-trace solutions leverage technologies like GPS, RFID, and IoT sensors to provide real-time monitoring of shipments, identify bottlenecks, and enable proactive issue resolution. This level of visibility allows businesses to optimize inventory positioning, anticipate disruptions, and maintain smooth operations.

While technology offers tremendous benefits to inventory management, businesses must also address challenges such as data security and integration. As more data is generated and shared within and outside the organization, ensuring data privacy and protecting against cyber threats is crucial. Integration of different technology systems, such as inventory management systems, ERP systems, and third-party applications, requires careful planning and execution to ensure smooth data flow and operational efficiency.

In summary, technology continues to evolve and revolutionize inventory management practices. Adopting the right technology solutions can help businesses optimize their inventory, improve accuracy, reduce costs, and enhance customer satisfaction. As technology continues to advance, businesses should stay updated with the latest trends and innovations in inventory management to leverage the full potential of technology and gain a competitive edge in the market.

———

Forecasting and Demand Planning

Forecasting and demand planning are critical aspects of inventory management that help businesses anticipate future demand for their products and plan their inventory accordingly. By accurately predicting customer demand, businesses can optimize their inventory levels, reduce costs, and enhance customer satisfaction.

1. Importance of Forecasting and Demand Planning

Forecasting and demand planning play essential roles in the success of businesses, enabling them to make informed decisions and effectively manage their inventory. Here's why these processes are crucial:

1.1 Anticipating Customer Demand: Forecasting allows businesses to estimate the demand for their products over a specific period. By leveraging past sales data, market trends, economic indicators, and other relevant factors, businesses can better predict future demand patterns.

1.2 Strategic Decision-Making: Accurate forecasting and demand planning enable businesses to make informed decisions about inventory levels, production, procurement, and supply chain management. This helps them align their resources, optimize operations, and meet customer demand effectively.

1.3 Minimizing Stockouts and Overstocking: By understanding future demand, businesses can ensure they have the right amount of inventory available without running out or overstocking. This reduces the risk of stockouts, improves customer satisfaction, and minimizes the costs associated with excess inventory.

1.4 Optimizing Inventory Turnover: Effective forecasting and demand planning allow businesses to maintain optimal inventory levels, reducing holding costs and improving inventory turnover. This leads to better cash flow management and increased profitability.

2. Factors Affecting Demand

To accurately forecast future demand, businesses must consider various factors that influence customer buying patterns. Some essential factors to consider include:

2.1 Historical Sales Data: Analyzing past sales data helps identify trends, seasonality, and demand fluctuations, providing insights into future demand patterns.

2.2 Market Trends: Studying market trends, such as changing consumer preferences, emerging technologies, and competitive landscape, helps businesses anticipate shifts in demand.

2.3 Economic Indicators: Factors like GDP growth, inflation rates, and employment rates impact consumer purchasing power, directly influencing product demand.

2.4 Seasonality: Many industries experience seasonal fluctuations in demand due to holidays, weather conditions, or cultural events. Understanding seasonal patterns is crucial for accurate demand planning.

2.5 Promotions and Marketing Campaigns: Sales promotions, discounts, and marketing campaigns can significantly impact customer demand. Evaluating the impact of such activities helps businesses adjust their forecasts accordingly.

2.6 Social and Demographic Factors: Social and demographic factors, such as population growth, age distribution, and cultural changes, can influence consumer behavior and demand for specific products.

2.7 External Events: Unforeseen events like natural disasters, geopolitical tensions, or public health crises can disrupt supply chains and significantly impact demand. Monitoring external events is crucial for adjusting forecasts and planning inventory accordingly.

3. Forecasting Methods

Several forecasting methods exist, each suited to different scenarios and data types. The following are commonly used methods:

3.1 Moving Average: This method calculates the average of a set number of previous periods to predict future demand. It is useful for stable demand patterns with minimal seasonality or trends.

3.2 Exponential Smoothing: Exponential smoothing assigns more weight to recent data and adjusts the forecast based on the level of smoothing parameter selected. It is suitable for demand patterns with trending or seasonal components.

3.3 Trend Projection: Trend projection extrapolates historical data to estimate future demand based on the observed trend. It is useful for identifying long-term demand patterns and predicting growth or decline in customer demand.

3.4 Regression Analysis: Regression analysis involves identifying relationships between dependent and independent variables to predict future demand accurately. This method is beneficial when several factors impact demand simultaneously.

3.5 Time Series Forecasting: Time series forecasting uses historical data to identify patterns, seasonality, and trends, enabling businesses to forecast future demand accurately. It involves techniques like exponential smoothing, moving averages, and autoregressive integrated moving average (ARIMA).

3.6 Machine Learning and Artificial Intelligence: Advanced techniques like machine learning and artificial intelligence are increasingly being employed for demand forecasting. These methods can handle large datasets and identify complex patterns in customer behavior, leading to more accurate forecasts.

3.7 Ensemble Forecasting: Ensemble forecasting combines the forecasts generated by multiple models or methods to improve accuracy. It leverages the strengths of individual methods and minimizes the impact of any individual forecast error.

4. Collaborative Planning, Forecasting, and Replenishment (CPFR)

Collaborative planning, forecasting, and replenishment (CPFR) is an approach that promotes collaboration and information sharing between businesses and their supply chain partners. Through CPFR, businesses can create more accurate forecasts and streamline the inventory planning process. Here's how CPFR works:

4.1 Information Sharing: Businesses share sales and inventory data, promotional plans, and other relevant information with their supply chain partners using advanced software platforms or through direct collaboration.

4.2 Joint Business Planning: Businesses and their partners collectively develop sales and inventory plans based on shared data and insights, aiming to align supply with expected demand.

4.3 Advanced Analytics and Algorithms: CPFR leverages advanced analytics and algorithms to analyze shared data, identify patterns, and generate accurate demand forecasts. This data-driven approach improves forecasting accuracy and enhances supply chain efficiency.

4.4 Promotional and Event Planning: CPFR helps businesses synchronize their promotional and event planning across the supply chain. By aligning marketing and sales strategies, businesses can meet increased demand during promotional periods without stockouts or excess inventory.

4.5 Demand Collaboration: Continuous communication and collaboration between businesses and their partners allow both parties to adjust plans based on actual demand and insights from the marketplace. This iterative process helps refine forecasts and optimize inventory levels.

4.6 Vendor Managed Inventory (VMI): VMI is a CPFR strategy where the supplier manages the inventory levels at the customer's location. The supplier continuously monitors stock levels and replenishes inventory as needed, based on collaborative demand planning and real-time data.

5. Demand Planning Tools and Software

Utilizing advanced tools and software can significantly enhance the accuracy and efficiency of forecasting and demand planning. Here are some commonly used demand planning software features and functionalities:

5.1 Data Integration: Demand planning software integrates data from various sources, such as sales records, promotions, external market data, and supplier information, to provide a comprehensive view of demand.

5.2 Statistical Modeling: Demand planning software employs advanced statistical models and algorithms to analyze historical data, identify patterns, and generate accurate demand forecasts.

5.3 Demand Collaboration Platform: Collaborative demand planning tools enable businesses to share data and collaborate with their supply chain partners, improving forecast accuracy and alignment.

5.4 Automatic Forecast Updates: Demand planning software automatically updates forecasts based on real-time sales data, enabling businesses to respond to changes in demand quickly.

5.5 Scenario Planning and What-If Analysis: These features allow businesses to simulate different demand scenarios, assess the impact of changes in variables, and make informed decisions about inventory planning and allocation.

5.6 Machine Learning and Artificial Intelligence: Demand planning software can leverage machine learning and artificial intelligence algorithms to continuously learn from new data, identify patterns, and improve forecast accuracy over time.

6. Adjusting for Forecast Error

While forecasting provides valuable insights, it may not always be 100% accurate. To mitigate the impact of forecast error, businesses can employ the following strategies:

6.1 Safety Stock6.1 Safety Stock: Safety stock is an additional inventory buffer that businesses maintain to mitigate the risk of stockouts due to forecast error or unexpected spikes in demand. By holding safety stock, businesses can ensure they have enough inventory to meet customer demand even if the forecast falls short.

6.2 Revising Forecasts: Businesses should regularly review and revise their forecasts based on actual sales data and feedback from customers and partners. This allows them to identify and correct any discrepancies or errors in the initial forecast.

6.3 Continuous Improvement: Forecasting is an iterative process, and businesses should continuously work towards improving their forecasting accuracy. They can achieve this by incorporating new data sources, refining forecasting models, and leveraging advanced analytics techniques.

6.4 Monitoring Key Performance Indicators (KPIs): By tracking KPIs like forecast accuracy, stockout rates, and lead time, businesses can assess the effectiveness of their forecasting and demand planning processes. These metrics provide insights into areas that require improvement and guide future decision-making.

6.5 Demand Sensing: Demand sensing involves using real-time data and analytics to detect changes in customer demand patterns. By monitoring factors like social media trends, customer reviews, and market indicators, businesses can adjust their forecasts and inventory plans accordingly.

6.6 Collaboration with Suppliers: Collaborating and sharing information with suppliers can help businesses better align their inventory levels with actual demand. This allows for more accurate replenishment planning and reduces the risk of excess inventory or stockouts.

6.7 Feedback Loops: Creating feedback loops between forecasting and other areas, such as sales, marketing, and operations, can help businesses gather feedback on the accuracy of their forecasts. This feedback can be used to refine future forecasts and improve overall accuracy.

6.8 Continuous Learning: Businesses should continuously learn from past forecasting errors and adjust their processes accordingly. This may involve investing in training, adopting new technologies, or seeking external expertise to improve forecasting accuracy.

In conclusion, forecasting and demand planning play a crucial role in inventory management. By accurately predicting future demand, businesses can optimize their inventory levels, reduce costs, and enhance customer satisfaction. Leveraging the right forecasting methods, collaborating with supply chain partners, and utilizing advanced demand planning tools and software can significantly improve forecasting accuracy and enable businesses to make informed decisions about their inventory.

Implementing Lean Principles in Inventory Control

Implementing Lean Principles in Inventory Control

In today's competitive business environment, organizations are constantly seeking ways to improve their operational efficiency and reduce waste. Lean principles, derived from the Toyota Production System, provide a comprehensive framework for achieving these goals. When applied to inventory control, lean principles can help streamline processes, optimize inventory levels, and drive sustainable improvements.

1. Understanding Lean Principles:

At the core of lean thinking is the drive to eliminate waste in all forms, including excess inventory. Lean principles focus on providing value to customers while minimizing non-value-added activities. Organizations that embrace lean principles aim to enhance productivity, reduce lead times, improve quality, and optimize their use of resources.

Lean identifies eight types of waste that can occur in inventory control processes:

a. Overproduction: Producing more than what is required by the customer or producing too early, leading to excess inventory. Overproduction is often caused by inaccurate forecasts, outdated demand patterns, or inefficient production scheduling.

b. Waiting: Delays caused by inefficiencies in the production or supply chain, leading to idle inventory. Waiting times can arise from lengthy setup times, limited visibility of demand, unpredictable lead times from suppliers, or bottlenecks in production.

c. Transportation: Unnecessary movement of materials or products, resulting in longer lead times and increased inventory. Excessive transportation can occur due to poor layout design, inefficient material handling processes, or lack of coordination between different operational areas.

d. Inventory: Excessive inventory levels that tie up capital and increase holding costs. This waste often stems from inaccurate demand forecasting, inadequate inventory control systems, or a lack of visibility throughout the supply chain.

e. Motion: Unnecessary movement of people or equipment, leading to inefficiencies in inventory handling. Inefficient layouts, disorganized storage areas, or excessive manual handling can contribute to wasted motion and potential errors.

f. Overprocessing: Performing more steps or activities than necessary, resulting in increased costs and potential defects. Overprocessing waste can arise from redundant quality checks, unnecessary inspections, or excessive packaging.

g. Defects: Quality issues that require rework or disposal, leading to wasted resources and additional inventory. Defects can be caused by poor process control, inadequate employee training, or insufficient quality assurance measures.

h. Unused employee creativity: Failing to tap into the knowledge and ideas of employees, thereby missing opportunities to improve inventory control processes. This waste can be addressed by implementing employee empowerment initiatives, promoting effective communication, and encouraging a culture of continuous improvement.

2. Value Stream Mapping:

Value stream mapping is a fundamental tool in lean principles that allows organizations to visually analyze their current inventory management processes. It helps identify areas of waste and inefficiency, facilitating targeted improvements. By mapping the flow of materials, information, and actions, organizations gain a holistic understanding of their inventory control processes. This enables the identification of non-value-added activities, bottlenecks, and areas of excess inventory.

Value stream mapping involves the following steps:

a. Identifying the product or service families: Categorize products or services into groups based on similar characteristics or process requirements. This helps in focusing on specific value streams and understanding the demand patterns associated with each product family.

b. Mapping the current state: With a cross-functional team, create a visual representation (often using symbols and diagrams) of the current inventory control processes, including information flow, material flow, and lead times. This visual depiction helps in understanding the sequence of activities, waiting times, and potential areas of waste.

c. Identifying areas of waste: Analyze the current state map to identify non-value-added activities, bottlenecks, and areas of excessive inventory. Engage the team in brainstorming ways to eliminate or reduce these wastes and improve efficiency.

d. Designing the future state: Using lean principles, develop a future state map that eliminates waste, reduces lead times, and optimizes inventory levels. This involves redesigning the inventory control processes to achieve a smoother flow of materials, improved visibility, and enhanced responsiveness to customer demand.

e. Implementing improvements: Develop an implementation plan and engage cross-functional teams in executing the identified improvements. Monitor the progress and evaluate the impact of changes made.

Value stream mapping is an ongoing process that organizations revisit periodically to ensure that the inventory control processes continue to align with customer needs and organizational objectives.

3. Batch Size Reduction:

Lean principles emphasize reducing batch sizes to achieve flexibility and responsiveness. Traditional large batch production leads to longer lead times, increased work-in-progress inventory, and a higher risk of obsolete inventory. By adopting smaller batch sizes, organizations can minimize inventory levels, lower holding costs, and reduce lead times.

Smaller, more frequent order quantities also enhance customer satisfaction by delivering products when they are needed, thus reducing the risk of stockouts or excess inventory. This level of responsiveness enables organizations to respond quickly to changes in demand patterns, minimize the risk of obsolescence, and maintain lean inventory levels.

Batch size reduction can be achieved through the following strategies:

a. Implementing a pull system: Instead of pushing products through the production process based on forecasts or arbitrary targets, organizations can adopt a pull system that produces products only in response to actual customer demand. This pull system can be supported by the use of Kanban cards or other visual signals.

b. Implementing just-in-time (JIT) production: JIT is a production strategy that aims to deliver finished products just in time to meet customer demand. By reducing batch sizes, maintaining close coordination with suppliers, and improving production flow, organizations can minimize inventory levels and reduce wasteful activities.

c. Implementing single-piece flow: Single-piece flow, also known as one-piece flow or continuous flow, involves producing items one at a time rather than in large batches. It ensures that each item moves continuously through the production process, reducing lead times, WIP inventory, and the risk of defects.

d. Implementing setup time reduction techniques: Setup time refers to the time required to prepare a machine or a production line for the production of a different product or variant. By implementing techniques like SMED (Single Minute Exchange of Die), organizations can significantly reduce setup times, enabling more frequent changeovers and smaller batch sizes.

4. Kanban System Implementation:

The kanban system, a visual signaling method, plays a pivotal role in lean inventory control. It allows organizations to manage inventory levels effectively and ensure the right amount of inventory is available at the right time.

The kanban system works by establishing visual signals that trigger replenishment when inventory levels reach a predefined threshold. By using kanban cards, bins, or electronic signals to authorize production or procurement, organizations can align inventory levels with actual demand. This approach minimizes excess inventory, reduces the risk of stockouts, and facilitates a smoother flow of materials throughout the supply chain.

There are different types of kanban systems that organizations can implement based on their specific needs:

a. Withdrawal kanban: This type of kanban is used to authorize the movement or withdrawal of inventory from one process to the next. When a downstream process requires more materials, the withdrawal kanban is triggered, indicating that it is time to withdraw materials from the preceding process.

b. Production kanban: This type of kanban signals the need to produce or replenish inventory. When a withdrawal kanban reaches the preceding process, it serves as an authorization to produce the required quantity of items.

c. Supplier kanban: In situations where organizations have external suppliers, the supplierkanban system can be implemented to manage the replenishment of materials or products from the supplier. When inventory levels reach a predefined threshold, a supplier kanban is triggered, signaling the need for the supplier to deliver more inventory.

Implementing a kanban system requires careful planning and coordination. The following steps can guide organizations in implementing a kanban system for inventory control:

a. Identify the value streams: Determine the flow of materials and the processes involved in the inventory control system. Identify the points where inventory needs to be replenished or moved to the next process.

b. Define inventory levels: Determine the optimal inventory levels for each process to ensure a smooth flow of materials and avoid stockouts or excess inventory. This can be determined based on lead times, demand patterns, and production capacities.

c. Establish kanban cards or signals: Decide on the visual signaling method that will be used to authorize inventory movement or replenishment. This could be physical kanban cards, electronic signals, or visual cues on bins or containers.

d. Set up kanban loops: Create the kanban loops by connecting the processes involved in the flow of materials. For each process, determine the number of kanban cards or signals that will be used to authorize inventory movement.

e. Implement tracking and monitoring systems: Establish systems to track and monitor the movement of kanban cards, inventory levels, and lead times. This will help identify any bottlenecks, delays, or issues in the kanban system, allowing for timely adjustments and improvements.

f. Train employees: Provide training to employees on how the kanban system works and their roles and responsibilities in maintaining the system. Ensure that everyone understands the importance of visual signals, timely replenishment, and the overall goal of reducing waste and optimizing inventory levels.

g. Continuously improve: Regularly review and evaluate the performance of the kanban system. Use the feedback from employees, customers, and suppliers to identify areas for improvement and implement changes as needed. Continuously monitor and adjust inventory levels, kanban loop sizes, and lead times to achieve optimal inventory control.

Implementing a kanban system requires a cultural shift towards a collaborative and synchronized approach to inventory control. It promotes transparency, cross-functional communication, and a focus on achieving the right inventory levels at the right time. By implementing a kanban system, organizations can significantly reduce waste, improve inventory turns, and enhance overall operational efficiency in their inventory control processes.

In conclusion, implementing lean principles in inventory control can lead to significant improvements in operational efficiency and reduction of waste. By understanding and addressing the different types of waste that can occur in inventory control processes, organizations can streamline their operations, optimize inventory levels, and improve customer satisfaction. Value stream mapping, batch size reduction, and kanban system implementation are key strategies that organizations can use to achieve lean inventory control and drive continuous improvement.

———

Managing Supplier Relationships and Procurement

In today's highly competitive business landscape, effectively managing supplier relationships and procurement is crucial for the success of any organization. This chapter delves into the key aspects of supplier management and the procurement process, providing deeper insights and strategies to optimize these functions.

1. The Importance of Supplier Relationships:

1.1 Strategic Supplier Relationships:
Developing strategic supplier relationships is vital for organizations to gain a competitive edge. Collaborating closely with key suppliers can lead to better integration of supply chain processes, joint value creation, and mutual long-term benefits. Strategic partnerships foster innovation, reduce costs, and enable organizations to respond more effectively to market dynamics.

1.2 Relationship Management Strategies:
To establish and nurture strong supplier relationships, organizations can adopt various strategies:

- Open and Transparent Communication: Maintaining clear and consistent lines of communication builds trust and facilitates effective collaboration. Regular meetings, performance reviews, and feedback mechanisms enable open dialogue between buyers and suppliers.

- Supplier Development Programs: Investing in supplier development programs can help suppliers enhance their capabilities and performance. Providing training, resources, and support can contribute to supplier growth and improve overall supply chain efficiency.

- Incentives and Reward Programs: Recognizing and rewarding suppliers for exceptional performance or cost-saving initiatives can reinforce positive behavior and encourage continuous improvement.

1.3 Supplier Segmentation:

Segmenting suppliers based on their strategic importance and impact on business performance allows organizations to allocate resources effectively. Supplier segmentation helps prioritize supplier development efforts, tailor relationship management strategies, and ensure alignment with organizational goals.

- Strategic Suppliers: These key suppliers have a high impact on the organization's operational efficiency and competitiveness. Close collaboration and mutual trust are crucial to maximize shared value and drive continuous improvement.

- Collaborative Suppliers: These suppliers have medium importance to the organization and involvement in joint initiatives, such as cost reduction or process improvement, can yield significant benefits.

- Transactional Suppliers: These suppliers have a low impact on the organization's operations and require minimal involvement beyond routine transactions. Streamlining processes and maintaining efficient communication channels with these suppliers is essential.

2. Supplier Evaluation and Selection:

2.1 Supplier Evaluation Criteria:

When evaluating potential suppliers, organizations should consider criteria tailored to their specific needs and goals. These criteria may include:

- Quality: Assessing a supplier's quality control processes, certifications, and track record to ensure consistent and reliable product/service delivery.

- Reliability: Evaluating a supplier's ability to meet delivery deadlines, maintain consistent supply, and provide responsive customer service.

- Pricing and Cost Structures: Analyzing pricing models, cost structures, and potential negotiation room to ensure competitive pricing and optimal cost management.

- Financial Stability: Assessing a supplier's financial health, market stability, and long-term viability to mitigate the risk of supply disruptions.

- Ethical Standards: Evaluating a supplier's adherence to ethical practices, social responsibility, and environmental sustainability.

- Innovation and Technology: Assessing a supplier's ability to provide innovative solutions, leverage technology advancements, and contribute to product/service development.

2.2 Supplier Performance Evaluation:
Implementing a robust supplier performance measurement system enables organizations to evaluate key metrics, including:

- On-time delivery: Monitoring a supplier's adherence to delivery schedules.

- Product Quality: Measuring the quality of supplied goods/services against predefined standards.

- Responsiveness: Assessing a supplier's agility and responsiveness in addressing issues, fulfilling urgent requests, and providing reliable support.

- Contractual Adherence: Evaluating how well a supplier complies with contractual terms and conditions.

- Innovation and Collaboration: Assessing a supplier's ability to provide innovative solutions, contribute to product/service development, and collaborate on continuous improvement initiatives.

2.3 Supplier Development:
Supplier development programs aim to improve supplier capabilities, performance, and overall supply chain efficiency. These programs may include:

- Training and Education: Offering training programs focused on specific areas, such as quality management, lean manufacturing, or sustainability, to help suppliers enhance their knowledge and skills.

- Sharing Best Practices: Facilitating the exchange of best practices among suppliers with similar challenges can drive continuous improvement across the supplier network.

- Joint Process Improvement Initiatives: Collaborating with suppliers to identify and implement process improvement opportunities helps streamline operations, reduce costs, and enhance overall supply chain performance.

3. Collaborative Supplier Relationships:

3.1 Joint Planning and Forecasting:
Collaborative planning and forecasting activities involve sharing vital information, such as demand forecasts, production plans, and market insights. This joint effort helps suppliers align their capabilities with customer requirements, anticipate demand fluctuations, and

optimize inventory levels, resulting in improved efficiency and reduced costs.

3.2 Supplier Relationship Management (SRM) Tools:

Leveraging technology-driven SRM tools can streamline and enhance supplier collaboration. These tools facilitate real-time communication, document sharing, performance tracking, and contract management. By centralizing supplier-related data and automating processes, organizations can improve transparency, efficiency, and decision-making.

3.3 Incentive Programs and Relationship-Building Activities:

To strengthen supplier relationships, organizations can implement incentive programs and engage in relationship-building activities. These may include supplier recognition events, joint problem-solving exercises, and regular face-to-face meetings. Such initiatives create an environment of trust, foster positive collaboration, and encourage suppliers to go the extra mile.

3.4 Long-Term Agreements and Contracts:

Establishing long-term agreements or contracts with key suppliers can provide stability and benefits for both parties. These agreements can include clauses for price adjustments, performance metrics, and continuous improvement, ensuring a mutually beneficial partnership.

4. Effective Procurement Processes:

4.1 Strategic Sourcing:

Strategic sourcing involves analyzing the overall supply chain to identify opportunities for cost reduction, risk mitigation, and process improvement. It includes activities such as supplier market research, negotiation tactics, and long-term relationship building to optimize sourcing decisions.

4.2 Supplier Diversity:

Promoting supplier diversity by engaging with a diverse range of suppliers contributes to organizational growth while fostering social inclusivity. Supplier diversity programs create opportunities for minority-owned, women-owned, and small businesses, encouraging innovation, economic development, and community support.

4.3 E-Procurement and Automation:

Leveraging e-procurement platforms and automation tools streamlines the procurement process, reducing manual effort and enhancing efficiency. These technologies enable electronic requisitioning, digital approvals, electronic RFQs, and automated supplier performance tracking.

4.4 Total Cost of Ownership (TCO) Analysis:
While cost is a crucial factor in procurement decisions, considering the total cost of ownership is essential. Taking into account factors such as acquisition costs, operating costs, maintenance costs, and end-of-life disposal costs helps make more informed sourcing decisions, optimizing value rather than solely focusing on upfront pricing.

5. Mitigating Supplier Risks:

5.1 Supply Chain Mapping and Redundancy:
Understanding the entire supply chain and mapping supplier dependencies helps identify areas prone to risks. Developing contingency plans and establishing backup suppliers mitigates potential disruptions and ensures business continuity.

5.2 Supply Chain Disruption Management:
Implementing proactive supply chain disruption management strategies allows organizations to minimize the impact of unforeseen events. These strategies include diversifying supplier sources, maintaining safety stock, and fostering flexibility in production and logistics.

5.3 Risk Monitoring and Early Warning Systems:
Utilizing advanced analytics and real-time monitoring systems can enable organizations to detect and respond to potential supplier risks promptly. Early warning systems provide insight into indicators such as financial instability, production issues, or regulatory non-compliance5.4 Supplier Performance Tracking:
Regularly monitoring supplier performance helps identify potential risks and areas for improvement. Key performance indicators (KPIs) can include on-time delivery, product quality, responsiveness, and compliance with contractual agreements. Tracking trends and analyzing data enables organizations to take proactive measures to address any performance issues.

5.5 Supplier Audits and Assessments:
Conducting supplier audits and assessments allows organizations to evaluate supplier processes, capabilities, and adherence to quality standards. These audits can be carried out through on-site visits, inspections, and documentation reviews. By assessing supplier performance and compliance, organizations can identify any gaps and work collaboratively with their suppliers to close them.

5.6 Supplier Relationship Contingency Plans:
Having contingency plans in place for supplier disruptions is crucial. Organizations should establish protocols and procedures to manage alternative sourcing, expedited deliveries, and communication channels in case of emergencies. These plans should be regularly updated and communicated to relevant stakeholders to ensure readiness during

disruptions.

6. Continuous Improvement in Supplier Management and Procurement:

6.1 Performance Reviews and Feedback:
Regular performance reviews provide an opportunity to assess supplier performance, identify areas for improvement, and provide feedback. These reviews should be conducted in a constructive and transparent manner, promoting open dialogue and alignment of goals.

6.2 Benchmarking and Best Practices:
Benchmarking supplier performance against industry standards and best practices helps identify improvement opportunities. Sharing benchmarking insights and best practices with suppliers can encourage collaboration and the adoption of innovative solutions.

6.3 Data Analytics and Technology:
Leveraging data analytics and technology-driven solutions can provide valuable insights into supplier performance, market trends, and cost optimization opportunities. Advanced analytics can help organizations make data-driven decisions, enhance visibility, and drive process efficiency.

6.4 Continuous Education and Training:
Keeping procurement and supply chain professionals updated with the latest industry trends, best practices, and technological advancements is essential. Investing in continuous education and training programs ensures that employees are equipped with the necessary knowledge and skills to effectively manage supplier relationships and procurement processes.

6.5 Cross-Functional Collaboration:
Promoting cross-functional collaboration among departments, such as procurement, supply chain, and finance, fosters a holistic approach to supplier management. By aligning goals, sharing information, and collaborating on joint initiatives, organizations can maximize the value derived from supplier relationships and procurement activities.

In summary, managing supplier relationships and procurement plays a vital role in the success of organizations. Establishing strategic supplier relationships, implementing effective evaluation and selection processes, and fostering collaborative partnerships can drive innovation, reduce costs, and enhance operational efficiency. By continuously improving supplier management practices and leveraging technology-driven solutions, organizations can optimize procurement processes, mitigate risks, and achieve long-term competitive advantage.

Warehouse Organization and Layout Optimization

Effective warehouse organization and layout optimization are essential for ensuring efficient operations and maximizing productivity. A well-organized warehouse not only improves order fulfillment speed but also reduces errors and minimizes the risk of accidents. In this chapter, we will explore various strategies and best practices for organizing and optimizing your warehouse layout.

1. Analyzing Space Requirements:
Before designing or optimizing your warehouse layout, it is important to conduct a thorough analysis of your space requirements. This process involves considering the volumes and characteristics of your inventory, such as size, weight, and fragility. It is also crucial to take into account factors like the velocity of movement, storage requirements (e.g., bulk storage, rack shelving, or specialized areas), and the need for different climate conditions (if applicable).

To accurately assess your space requirements, you can employ techniques like ABC analysis, which categorizes items based on their demand and value. This analysis helps determine how to allocate space effectively, ensuring that frequently accessed items are located in easily accessible areas while slower-moving goods are stored in less active regions.

2. Design Principles:
When organizing your warehouse, certain design principles can be applied to improve efficiency and productivity. These principles include:

- Establishing a logical flow: One of the fundamental principles of warehouse design is to arrange your warehouse layout in a way that facilitates a smooth and logical flow of products. This flow should begin from the receiving area, move to storage, order picking, packaging, and finally, shipping. By separating different functional areas and implementing clear pathways for material handling equipment, you can ensure that goods move efficiently through your warehouse.

- Minimizing travel distances: Travel distance plays a significant role in warehouse efficiency. By minimizing the distance traveled by workers and equipment, you can reduce the time required to pick, pack, and ship orders. To achieve this, place frequently accessed items closer to the shipping or packing areas. Group products with high demand near the picking area and reserve appropriate space for slower-moving items. This strategic placement minimizes unnecessary travel, maximizes productivity, and improves order fulfillment speed.

- Utilizing vertical space: Warehouses often have a significant amount of vertical space that can be leveraged to optimize storage capacity. By installing high shelving or racks, you can effectively use this vertical space to store items that are not frequently accessed. This frees up valuable floor space for more active and faster-moving items. Additionally, you can implement mezzanine levels or multi-tier racking systems to further maximize storage capacity within your warehouse.

- Implementing zoning: Dividing your warehouse into zones based on product attributes, order types, or other relevant criteria is an effective strategy for improving operational efficiency. This zoning strategy allows for more accurate and efficient picking, packing, and restocking processes. For example, you can have separate zones for high-demand products, slow-moving items, specialized storage requirements (e.g., perishables, hazardous materials), and even dedicated areas for value-added services like assembly or customization. Implementing zone labeling and signage can assist workers in navigating the warehouse effectively, saving time and reducing errors.

3. Equipment and Material Handling Considerations:
Choosing the right equipment and material handling solutions is crucial for warehouse optimization. Factors to consider include:

- Forklifts and other machinery: Selecting appropriate and well-maintained machinery that meets the requirements of your warehouse is essential. Consider factors such as lifting capacity, maneuverability, energy efficiency, and adaptability to different storage systems. It is vital to ensure that your material handling equipment is regularly inspected, serviced, and operated by trained professionals to prevent accidents and maintain operational efficiency.

- Conveyor systems: Implementing conveyor systems can significantly enhance picking and packing operations. By automating the movement of goods between different areas of your warehouse, you can significantly reduce the time and effort required for manual transportation. Analyze your order volume and flow to determine the type and configuration of conveyors that will best suit your warehouse needs. Consider factors like roller conveyors for cartons, belt conveyors for loose items, and even overhead conveyor systems for specific applications.

- Automated systems: Automating certain warehouse operations can revolutionize efficiency and accuracy. Evaluate the feasibility of incorporating automation into your warehouse, such as robotic systems and automated storage and retrieval systems (AS/RS). These systems can improve speed, accuracy, and productivity in tasks like picking, order consolidation, inventory management, and replenishment. Assess the cost-benefit analysis and ensure that your warehouse management system (WMS) can seamlessly integrate with automated systems.

4. Safety Considerations:
Maintaining a safe working environment is of utmost importance to protect both your employees and inventory. Ensure that safety measures are integrated into your warehouse layout. Consider the following:

- Well-defined walkways: Clearly mark pedestrian pathways separate from material handling equipment routes to prevent accidents. Implement physical barriers like guardrails and bollards to further enhance safety.

- Adequate signage: Use clear and visible signage throughout the warehouse to indicate emergency exits, hazardous areas, and safety precautions. Floor markings can also help guide workers and promote safety awareness.

- Proper lighting: Well-lit warehouses promote better visibility, reduce the chances of accidents, and enhance overall productivity. Ensure that all areas of your warehouse, including aisles, storage areas, and packing stations, have adequate lighting.

- Fire safety: Install appropriate fire safety equipment, such as fire extinguishers, fire alarms, and sprinkler systems. Regularly inspect and maintain these systems to ensure their effectiveness. Proper ventilation systems should also be in place to mitigate the risk of fire hazards and improve air quality within the warehouse.

- Employee training: Effective safety measures go hand in hand with proper training. Ensure that all employees are trained in safety protocols, including proper lifting techniques, equipment operation, and emergency procedures. Conduct regular safety training sessions and incentivize employees to follow safety guidelines.

5. Continuous Improvement:
Warehouse organization and layout optimization should be an ongoing process. Regularly assess your operations, gather feedback from employees, and consider implementing improvements based on changing business needs. Continuously strive for better efficiency and adaptability to keep up with evolving market demands.

Evaluate key performance metrics such as order fulfillment rate, order accuracy, inventory turnover, and cycle time to identify areas that require improvement. Analyze customer feedback, order patterns, and industry trends to identify areas where warehouse operations can be further enhanced. Review the effectiveness of your layout and make adjustments accordingly. Stay updated with new technologies and industry best practices to stay ahead in a competitive market.

By implementing effective warehouse organization and layout optimization strategies, you can enhance operational efficiency, minimize errors, and maximize productivity. This chapter provided an extended overview of key considerations and best practices to help you create a well-organized and optimized warehouse environment. Remember to tailor these principles to suit your specific business requirements and to regularly evaluate and adjust your warehouse operations to maintain a competitive edge.

———————

Inventory Accuracy and Cycle Counting

In the world of inventory management, accuracy is crucial. A small deviation in inventory levels can have a significant impact on customer satisfaction, production schedules, and financial performance. That's why maintaining inventory accuracy plays a vital role in the success of any organization.

Inventory accuracy refers to the alignment between recorded inventory levels and actual physical stock present in the warehouse. Achieving high inventory accuracy ensures that inventory counts are reliable and up-to-date.

One of the most common and effective methods used to maintain inventory accuracy is through a process called cycle counting. Cycle counting involves counting a portion of the inventory on a regular basis throughout the year, rather than conducting a full physical inventory count all at once. This approach allows for more frequent verification of stock levels and reduces the disruption caused by a complete shutdown for a physical inventory count.

Implementing an effective cycle counting program requires careful planning and execution. Here are some key steps to consider:

1. Item Classification: Classify your inventory items based on their value, demand, and criticality. This classification provides a basis for prioritizing cycle counts. The ABC classification method is commonly used, with Category A representing high-value items that require more frequent counting due to their financial impact. Category B represents moderately valued items, and Category C represents low-value items that may be counted less frequently. Additionally, consider incorporating a classification based on item characteristics, such as perishability, seasonality, or risk of obsolescence, to further prioritize cycle counts.

2. Cycle Count Frequency: Determine the frequency at which each item or group of items should be counted. High-value items or fast-moving items may require more frequent

counts than low-value or slow-moving items. Factors such as demand volatility, lead time, and historical accuracy can also guide the decision-making process. Furthermore, analyze historical data and identify any patterns of discrepancies or inaccuracies to inform the frequency of cycle counts. For example, items with a history of frequent discrepancies may warrant more frequent counts.

3. Counting Methodology: Select a counting methodology that suits your inventory and operational needs. Common methods include physical counts, barcode scanning, or using inventory management software. Each method has its advantages and limitations. Physical counts involve manually counting items, while barcode scanning improves data accuracy and reduces human error but requires the appropriate infrastructure and equipment. Inventory management software provides real-time visibility into stock levels and automates the counting process, but it requires integration with the existing systems and accurate data entry. Determine the optimal method or combination of methods based on the nature of your inventory, resources available, and desired level of accuracy.

4. Cycle Count Scheduling: Plan the cycle counting schedule in advance to ensure even coverage throughout the year. Avoid peak operational periods when inventory movements are high, as this may lead to discrepancies. Depending on the volume and complexity of your inventory, you may decide to conduct daily, weekly, monthly, or quarterly cycle counts. Strive for a consistent and balanced approach, spreading the counts across different product categories and locations. Consider incorporating a rotating schedule to ensure that all items are consistently counted over time.

5. Allocation of Resources: Allocate adequate resources, such as trained staff or technology, to conduct cycle counts efficiently and accurately. Ensure that the designated personnel understand the counting process and any special handling or identification requirements. Provide training and clear instructions to minimize discrepancies and improve overall accuracy. Consider leveraging technology solutions, such as mobile devices with barcode scanning capabilities or RFID technology, to streamline the counting process. With the right resources in place, you can minimize the time and effort required for cycle counts while maximizing accuracy.

6. Documentation and Investigation: Document and investigate any discrepancies found during cycle counts. Determine the root causes, such as inaccuracies in receiving, picking, or data entry, and take necessary corrective actions to prevent future errors. Root cause analysis can reveal patterns and systemic issues that require attention. Regular review and analysis of discrepancy reports help identify trends and facilitate continuous improvement. Additionally, consider implementing a robust system for documenting and tracking inventory adjustments resulting from the cycle counting process. This ensures transparency and accountability in inventory management practices.

7. Continuous Improvement: Regularly review and evaluate the cycle counting process to identify areas for improvement. Analyze trends, monitor the effectiveness of corrective actions, and adjust the cycle counting program accordingly. Solicit feedback from stakeholders involved in the inventory management process, including warehouse personnel, procurement teams, and customers, if possible. Their input can provide valuable insights into potential areas of improvement. Leverage data analytics and inventory management software to gain insights and make data-driven decisions. By analyzing cycle count data, you can identify patterns, identify areas of improvement, and optimize inventory accuracy.

By implementing an accurate cycle counting process, organizations can maintain higher inventory accuracy levels, improve order fulfillment rates, reduce stockouts, and maximize working capital efficiency. It also helps identify potential issues such as theft, damage, or obsolete inventory in a timely manner, allowing for proactive measures to be taken. Continuous monitoring and improvement of inventory accuracy support operational excellence and customer satisfaction.

Remember, maintaining inventory accuracy and conducting cycle counts should be a continuous effort to ensure inventory levels remain in sync with the records. An accurate inventory management system positively impacts the entire supply chain, ultimately contributing to strategic decision-making and long-term profitability.

———————

Effective Inventory Replenishment Strategies

Effective Inventory Replenishment Strategies

Inventory replenishment is a crucial aspect of inventory management that directly impacts the availability of products to meet customer demands. Without an effective replenishment strategy, businesses may experience stockouts, excess inventory, and inefficient use of resources. In this chapter, we will explore various strategies that can help businesses optimize their inventory replenishment processes.

1. Just-in-Time (JIT) Inventory Replenishment: Just-in-Time is a widely adopted inventory management strategy that aims to minimize inventory levels by synchronizing production and supplier deliveries with customer demand. By implementing JIT, businesses can reduce carrying costs, minimize waste, and improve overall operational efficiency. However, this strategy requires accurate demand forecasting and strong supplier relationships to ensure timely deliveries.

JIT relies heavily on accurate demand forecasting to ensure that inventory is replenished just in time to meet customer demand. By leveraging historical sales data, market trends, and other relevant factors, businesses can develop reliable demand forecasts that support JIT practices. Additionally, establishing strong relationships with suppliers is crucial for JIT success. Close collaboration allows businesses to provide suppliers with real-time sales data, enabling them to align their production and delivery schedules to meet fluctuating demands effectively. JIT can also be enhanced through vendor-managed inventory (VMI) partnerships, where suppliers take responsibility for monitoring and replenishing inventory based on agreed-upon inventory levels.

2. Economic Order Quantity (EOQ) Model: The EOQ model is a mathematical formula that helps determine the ideal order quantity to minimize holding costs and ordering costs. By analyzing factors such as demand, ordering costs, and carrying costs, businesses can calculate the optimal order quantity that balances the costs associated with holding excess inventory and ordering too frequently.

To calculate the EOQ, businesses need to gather data on demand patterns, unit costs, ordering costs, and holding costs. The EOQ formula takes into account these variables to determine the optimal order quantity that minimizes holding and ordering costs. Businesses can set reorder points based on the EOQ to trigger replenishment orders, ensuring a continuous flow of inventory. However, it is essential to periodically review and adjust the EOQ due to changes in factors such as demand variability, carrying costs, and supplier lead times.

3. ABC Analysis: ABC analysis is a method that categorizes inventory items based on their value and importance. It classifies items into three categories - A, B, and C - based on their contribution to sales revenue. A-categorized items are high-value and high-demand, B-categorized items have moderate value and demand, while C-categorized items are low-value and low-demand. By focusing efforts on managing A-categorized items more closely, businesses can prioritize inventory replenishment and ensure the availability of their most valuable products.

ABC analysis helps businesses identify inventory items that require different levels of attention, allowing for more efficient inventory management. By prioritizing A-categorized items, businesses can ensure that they have enough stock to satisfy customer demand. Moreover, they can implement more frequent replenishment or safety stock strategies for A-items since they contribute significantly to sales revenue. B and C items, on the other hand, may require less frequent replenishment or alternate inventory management strategies to minimize costs. C-categorized items with minimal contribution to sales revenue may be prime candidates for sourcing through dropshipping or consignment inventory to reduce storage costs.

4. Vendor-Managed Inventory (VMI): VMI is a collaborative approach where suppliers are responsible for monitoring and replenishing inventory at their customers' locations. By sharing real-time inventory data and creating mutual visibility into the supply chain, this strategy allows suppliers to optimize their production and delivery schedules, ensuring on-time replenishment while reducing carrying costs for businesses. VMI also strengthens supplier-customer relationships by fostering trust and shared goals.

VMI relies on a strong partnership between suppliers and customers. Through the exchange of real-time inventory data, suppliers gain better visibility into customer demands and inventory levels. This enables them to take proactive measures to replenish inventory, avoiding stockouts and ensuring optimal inventory levels for the customer. On the other side, customers benefit from reduced inventory carrying costs, as they no longer have to maintain excess stock. VMI also helps reduce lead times and improve order fulfillment, enhancing overall customer satisfaction.

5. Safety Stock: Safety stock refers to an extra quantity of inventory that is held as a buffer

to absorb unexpected variations in demand or supply disruptions. By maintaining safety stock levels, businesses can prevent stockouts and meet customer demands more consistently. The appropriate amount of safety stock should be determined based on factors like lead time, demand variability, and customer service level objectives.

Calculating the appropriate safety stock level requires considering various factors. These include lead time uncertainty, demand variability, desired service levels, and cost implications. By conducting thorough analysis and utilizing statistical techniques such as demand forecasting and probability distributions, businesses can determine an appropriate safety stock level for each inventory item. Safety stock strategies can be refined further by implementing technologies like agile supply chain systems or integrating predictive analytics to enhance demand forecasting accuracy.

6. Continuous Replenishment: Continuous replenishment involves establishing real-time communication and collaboration between suppliers and customers to ensure a continuous flow of inventory. By sharing information regarding sales, inventory levels, and demand forecasts, businesses can enable automatic replenishment based on pre-defined parameters. This strategy helps minimize stockouts, reduce stock holding costs, and improve customer satisfaction by ensuring timely availability of products.

Continuous replenishment relies on efficient information sharing between suppliers and customers for successful implementation. Leveraging technology tools such as Electronic Data Interchange (EDI) or Application Programming Interfaces (APIs), businesses can establish real-time connectivity with their suppliers. This enables automatic replenishment triggered by predefined thresholds or order triggers. By continuously monitoring inventory levels and analyzing demand patterns, businesses can create a seamless flow of inventory, minimizing disruptions and optimizing stock levels. Continuous replenishment can be further enhanced through the adoption of advanced technologies like Internet of Things (IoT) sensors or RFID tags that enable real-time inventory tracking and automated replenishment processes.

7. Consignment Inventory: Consignment inventory is a practice where suppliers place their products at the customer's location, and ownership of the inventory remains with the supplier until it is consumed or sold. This strategy reduces the financial burden on the customer as they only pay for the consumed inventory, minimizing holding costs and reducing the risk of obsolete inventory.

Consignment inventory offers benefits to both suppliers and customers. Suppliers can reduce their inventory holding costs by keeping the inventory in customer locations instead of their own warehouses. Customers, in turn, benefit from reduced financial risk, as they only pay for the inventory once it is consumed or sold. This strategy enhances supply chain efficiency by minimizing inventory transfers and allowing customers to have immediate access to products while reducing their inventory carrying costs. Additionally, consignment inventory can support just-in-time practices, streamlining replenishment and reducing lead times.

8. Cross-Docking: Cross-docking is a logistics strategy that involves receiving products from suppliers and immediately sorting and redistributing them for outbound shipments without storing them in a warehouse. This approach streamlines inventory replenishment by eliminating the need for storage and reducing handling costs. Cross-docking requires close coordination with suppliers and efficient logistics systems to ensure timely and accurate product flow.

Cross-docking requires careful planning and coordination to ensure smooth operations. Suppliers must deliver the products to the cross-docking facility on time, and shipments must be efficiently sorted and combined to match outbound orders. Utilizing technology such as barcode scanning, automatedsorting systems, and real-time tracking can greatly improve the efficiency and accuracy of cross-docking operations. By reducing the time and costs associated with inventory storage, cross-docking enables businesses to replenish inventory quickly and avoid unnecessary holding costs.

9. Dropshipping: Dropshipping is a fulfillment method where businesses do not keep the products they sell in stock. Instead, when a customer places an order, the business purchases the products from a third-party supplier who then ships the products directly to the customer. This strategy eliminates the need for businesses to handle inventory or fulfill orders, reducing costs and streamlining the replenishment process.

Dropshipping offers several benefits for businesses. Firstly, it eliminates the need for businesses to invest in inventory storage or fulfillment infrastructure, reducing upfront costs and overhead expenses. Additionally, dropshipping allows businesses to offer a wide range of products without the need for physical inventory. By leveraging suppliers' inventory and fulfillment capabilities, businesses can quickly add new products to their offerings and respond to customer demands in a more agile manner. However, dropshipping does come with certain challenges, such as reliance on third-party suppliers and potential quality control issues. Therefore, it is essential for businesses to carefully select and maintain strong relationships with reputable suppliers to ensure reliable product quality and timely fulfillment.

10. Centralized Replenishment: Centralized replenishment involves consolidating the procurement and replenishment activities for multiple locations into a central location or team. In this approach, the central team handles the ordering and distribution of inventory to various locations based on their specific needs. By centralizing the replenishment process, businesses can benefit from economies of scale, improved visibility, and better control over inventory levels.

Centralized replenishment allows businesses to consolidate orders and negotiate better pricing and terms with suppliers. It also enables better coordination and planning of inventory distribution to multiple locations, minimizing stockouts and excess inventory. With centralized replenishment, businesses can leverage technology tools and analytics to gain visibility into inventory levels across multiple locations, allowing for more accurate demand forecasting and optimal order placement. However, it is crucial for businesses to consider the unique requirements and demand patterns of each location to ensure sufficient stock availability and minimize disruptions to operations.

In conclusion, effective inventory replenishment is essential for businesses to meet customer demands efficiently while optimizing inventory levels and costs. Implementing strategies such as just-in-time inventory replenishment, economic order quantity models, ABC analysis, vendor-managed inventory, safety stock management, continuous replenishment, consignment inventory, cross-docking, dropshipping, and centralized replenishment can help businesses streamline their replenishment processes and maintain optimal inventory levels. By carefully analyzing their specific requirements and utilizing the appropriate strategies, businesses can improve operational efficiency, minimize stockouts, and enhance customer satisfaction.

———

The Power of Data Analytics in Inventory Management

In today's fast-paced and highly competitive business environment, making informed decisions is crucial to the success of any organization. This is especially true in the field of inventory management, where effective management can significantly impact a company's profitability, customer satisfaction, and overall operational efficiency. To achieve these goals, businesses have begun harnessing the power of data analytics to obtain valuable insights and make data-driven decisions.

Data analytics, as a tool, has revolutionized inventory management due to advancements in technology and the increasing availability of vast amounts of data. By utilizing statistical methods, algorithms, and software, companies can analyze large volumes of data to identify patterns, trends, and correlations. This allows them to gain insights into various aspects of inventory control, optimize inventory levels, reduce costs, improve customer satisfaction, and enhance overall operational efficiency.

One of the primary areas where data analytics can be applied in inventory management is demand forecasting. Traditional demand forecasting methods often relied on simple historical sales data, leading to inaccuracies and inefficiencies. However, with data analytics, businesses can now analyze a multitude of variables including historical sales, customer behavior, economic indicators, seasonality, and promotions to develop accurate demand forecasts. These forecasts enable organizations to plan their inventory levels more effectively, minimizing the risk of stockouts or overstock situations.

Furthermore, by utilizing predictive analytics techniques, businesses can forecast short-term and long-term demand with greater accuracy. This allows for more proactive inventory management strategies such as initiating production or procurement processes well in advance to cater to anticipated demand. With accurate demand forecasts, companies can align their inventory levels with customer demand, reducing carrying costs and ensuring high customer service levels.

Supplier relationship management is another area where data analytics proves invaluable.

By analyzing data related to delivery times, order accuracy, pricing, and quality, companies can identify the most reliable and cost-effective suppliers. This analysis allows organizations to make informed decisions about supplier selection, negotiate better terms and pricing, and establish strategic partnerships. Collaborating closely with suppliers can result in reduced lead times, improved order accuracy, and increased supply chain visibility. These advancements lead to cost savings, minimized inventory holding costs, and enhanced overall supply chain efficiency.

Additionally, data analytics can help identify slow-moving or obsolete inventory items, allowing companies to take appropriate actions such as promotions, markdowns, or liquidation. By scrutinizing sales data, lead times, and other relevant variables, businesses can optimize order quantities and reorder points. This optimization ensures that stock levels are neither excessive nor insufficient, reducing carrying costs while maintaining high customer service levels.

Warehousing operations also benefit from data analytics. By analyzing data related to order picking times, storage utilization, and order accuracy, organizations can identify areas for improvement and implement changes to enhance operational efficiency. For instance, through data analytics, companies can determine the most efficient picking routes, the optimal storage locations for different products, and the need for reconfiguring the warehouse layout. These insights lead to reduced labor costs, increased throughput, and minimized errors, ultimately sharpening their competitive edge in the market.

It is important to note that harnessing the power of data analytics in inventory management necessitates the appropriate technology infrastructure and tools. This includes robust data management systems capable of handling large volumes of data, data visualization software to present insights in a user-friendly manner, and skilled analysts who can interpret the data and provide actionable insights. Investing in these resources and fostering a data-driven culture can yield significant benefits for organizations, such as improved decision-making, enhanced efficiency, and increased profitability.

Moreover, the integration of data analytics with other emerging technologies, such as the Internet of Things (IoT), allows companies to monitor inventory in real-time. By utilizing sensors, RFID tags, and connected devices, businesses can gather data on inventory levels, product movement, and environmental conditions. This real-time information enables proactive inventory management, minimizing stockouts and reducing the likelihood of product spoilage or damage. Combined with advanced analytics techniques, companies can leverage this data to optimize their inventory levels, streamline replenishment processes, and ensure seamless supply chain operations.

In conclusion, data analytics plays a pivotal role in modern inventory management. By leveraging the power of data and deploying advanced analytical techniques, companies can gain valuable insights into their inventory performance, improve demand forecasting accuracy, optimize supplier relationships, reduce costs, enhance overall operational efficiency, and future-proof their operations. Embracing data analytics in inventory management not only provides a competitive edge in today's complex business landscape but also helps organizations stay ahead of the curve and achieve sustainable growth. The ability to make data-driven decisions ensures that businesses can effectively navigate the challenges of inventory management and position themselves for long-term success in the market.

———

Performance Metrics and Continuous Improvement in Inventory Management

In the ever-evolving world of inventory management, it is crucial to establish and monitor performance metrics to drive continuous improvement. These metrics serve as objective measures to evaluate the effectiveness and efficiency of your inventory management practices. By tracking and analyzing these key performance indicators (KPIs), you can identify areas for improvement, make informed decisions, and optimize your inventory processes.

1. Inventory Turnover: Inventory turnover is a fundamental metric that measures how quickly your inventory is being sold and replaced over a specific period of time. It indicates how efficiently you are managing your inventory levels and how well you are meeting customer demand. A higher inventory turnover ratio typically suggests effective inventory management and minimizes the risk of obsolete or deadstock.

To calculate inventory turnover, divide the cost of goods sold (COGS) by the average inventory value during a given period. A higher turnover indicates that your inventory is being sold quickly, which helps generate cash flow and reduce carrying costs. However, it is essential to strike a balance, as excessive turnover might indicate a lack of inventory availability or missed sales opportunities.

2. Gross Margin Return on Investment (GMROI): GMROI is a metric that links inventory performance to profitability. It measures the return on investment (ROI) generated from the sale of inventory, taking into account both sales revenue and the cost of goods sold (COGS). By calculating GMROI, you can assess the profitability of your inventory investments and identify areas where adjustments may be required.

To calculate GMROI, divide the gross margin (sales revenue minus COGS) by the average inventory value during a given period, and then multiply it by 100. A higher GMROI indicates that your inventory investment is generating strong profitability. It helps measure the balance between sales revenue, inventory costs, and profit margins. Monitoring GMROI regularly enables you to evaluate the effectiveness of your inventory decisions and identify opportunities to optimize your product mix, pricing, and procurement strategies.

3. Fill Rate: Fill rate measures the percentage of customer orders that are completely filled from available inventory. It reflects your ability to meet customer demand promptly and accurately. A high fill rate indicates strong customer service and efficient inventory control, while a low fill rate may lead to dissatisfied customers and lost sales.

To calculate fill rate, divide the total number of complete orders by the total number of orders received, and then multiply it by 100. An ideal fill rate is generally considered to be above 95%. Monitoring fill rate allows you to identify potential issues in your order processing, inventory availability, or forecasting accuracy. By maintaining a high fill rate, you improve customer satisfaction, reduce order cancellations or returns, and enhance your reputation as a reliable supplier.

4. Order Accuracy: Order accuracy measures the percentage of orders that are processed correctly without errors or discrepancies. It ensures that the right items are shipped in the right quantities and to the right locations. Improving order accuracy reduces costly returns, customer complaints, and related operational inefficiencies.

To calculate order accuracy, divide the number of correctly processed orders by the total number of orders, and then multiply it by 100. Aim for an order accuracy rate close to 100%. Regularly monitoring order accuracy allows you to identify and address issues such as picking errors, misplacements, or system integration problems. Enhancing order accuracy not only improves customer satisfaction but also reduces unnecessary costs associated with incorrect shipments and reshipments.

5. Stockout Rate: The stockout rate measures the frequency of inventory stockouts or situations in which desired products are unavailable when customers request them. A high stockout rate indicates inadequate inventory forecasting, replenishment, or management, which can lead to lost sales, dissatisfied customers, and reduced profitability.

To calculate the stockout rate, divide the number of stockouts by the total number of customer orders, and then multiply it by 100. A stockout rate below 5% is generally desirable. By monitoring the stockout rate, you can identify patterns, plan for demand fluctuations, and optimize your inventory replenishment strategies. Minimizing stockouts improves customer satisfaction, maintains revenue streams, and enhances your brand's reliability.

6. On-Time Delivery: On-time delivery measures the percentage of customer orders that are delivered within the promised or expected delivery time frame. It directly impacts customer

satisfaction, loyalty, and overall business performance. Monitoring and improving on-time delivery can help mitigate stockouts, improve customer relationships, and gain a competitive advantage.

To calculate on-time delivery, divide the number of orders delivered on time by the total number of orders, and then multiply it by 100. Strive for an on-time delivery rate exceeding 95%. Analyzing on-time delivery metrics enables you to pinpoint potential bottlenecks in your supply chain, transportation, or fulfillment processes. By enhancing on-time delivery, you minimize order delays, strengthen customer trust, and differentiate yourself from your competitors.

7. Backorder Rate: The backorder rate measures the percentage of customer orders that cannot be fulfilled immediately due to insufficient inventory. It provides insights into the effectiveness of your inventory planning and replenishment processes. A high backorder rate may indicate the need for better inventory management strategies to prevent order delays and minimize customer dissatisfaction.

To calculate the backorder rate, divide the number of backorders by the total number of customer orders, and then multiply it by 100. Aim for a backorder rate below 5%. A high backorder rate calls for a reassessment of your demand forecasting, safety stock levels, and supply chain coordination. Reducing backorders enhances customer satisfaction, prevents lost sales, and improves overall operational efficiency.

8. Carrying Costs: Carrying costs refer to the expenses associated with storing and holding inventory over a specific timeframe. It includes costs such as warehousing, insurance, handling, depreciation, obsolescence, and financing. Monitoring and managing carrying costs are crucial to ensure adequate cash flow, optimize inventory levels, and improve profitability.

To calculate carrying costs, determine the average inventory value and multiply it by the carrying cost rate. The carrying cost rate usually includes factors like warehouse rent, utilities, insurance, interest rates, and taxes associated with inventory holding. By measuring carrying costs, you can identify opportunities to reduce expenses through more efficient inventory control, improved demand forecasting, and strategic partnerships with suppliers.

9. Perfect Order Rate: The perfect order rate measures the percentage of orders that are delivered to the customer without any errors or issues from start to finish. It encompasses various aspects such as order accuracy, on-time delivery, complete fulfillment, and adherence to customer requirements. Monitoring the perfect order rate provides you with a comprehensive view of your overall order fulfillment process and helps identify areas for improvement.

To calculate the perfect order rate, multiply the percentage of orders with order accuracy, on-time delivery, and complete fulfillment. Aim for a perfect order rate close to 100%. Monitoring the perfect order rate allows you to streamline your order fulfillment processes, minimize costs associated with order errors, improve customer satisfaction, and enhance your brand reputation.

Continuous improvement is a vital aspect of inventory management. By regularly reviewing and analyzing the performance metrics mentioned above, you can identify opportunities to improve efficiency, reduce costs, and enhance customer satisfaction. Implementing process enhancements, adopting advanced inventory management technologies, and fostering a culture of continuous improvement can lead to better inventory control, increased profitability, and a competitive edge in the market.

Remember, every business is unique, so it is essential to tailoryour performance metrics and continuous improvement efforts to your specific industry, business goals, and customer expectations. Regularly review and update your metrics to ensure they align with current market conditions and business objectives.

In addition to tracking and analyzing performance metrics, continuous improvement in inventory management also involves implementing best practices and adopting innovative approaches. Here are some strategies to consider:

1. Demand forecasting: Improve the accuracy of your demand forecasting by leveraging historical data, market trends, customer insights, and collaboration with sales and marketing teams. Use advanced forecasting techniques and software to optimize your inventory levels, avoid stockouts, and minimize excess inventory.

2. Supplier management: Establish strong relationships with your suppliers and regularly evaluate their performance. Monitor lead times, delivery reliability, quality, and pricing to ensure you have reliable and efficient supply chains. Consider implementing vendor scorecards and conducting regular supplier performance reviews.

3. Inventory optimization: Analyze your inventory levels and identify opportunities to optimize them. Implement inventory segmentation techniques to prioritize high-demand and high-margin products. Consider implementing just-in-time (JIT) or lean inventory management practices to minimize carrying costs and improve order fulfillment efficiency.

4. Warehouse layout and organization: Optimize your warehouse layout and organization to improve efficiency. Designate areas for fast-moving products, implement proper labeling and signage, and use inventory management tools like barcode scanners or RFID technology for accurate and streamlined inventory tracking. Implement efficient picking and packing processes to minimize errors and improve productivity.

5. Technology integration: Consider integrating inventory management software with other business systems such as ERP (Enterprise Resource Planning) or POS (Point of Sale) systems to ensure accurate and real-time inventory data. Use advanced analytics tools to gain insights into inventory trends, customer behavior, and supply chain performance.

6. Cross-functional collaboration: Foster collaboration between different departments such as sales, marketing, operations, and finance to ensure alignment and synergy in inventory management processes. Encourage open communication, information sharing, and joint decision-making to improve forecasting accuracy, demand planning, and order fulfillment.

7. Continuous training and education: Invest in ongoing training and education for your inventory management team. Keep them updated on the latest industry trends, technologies, and best practices. Encourage them to attend relevant conferences, seminars, or webinars to enhance their knowledge and skills.

By implementing these strategies and continuously monitoring and improving your performance metrics, you can optimize your inventory management practices, improve customer satisfaction, reduce costs, and gain a competitive advantage in the market. Remember, inventory management is an ongoing process, and continuous improvement is key to staying ahead in a rapidly changing business environment.

The Importance of Collaboration in Inventory Management

In today's fast-paced and ever-evolving business landscape, effective collaboration has emerged as a crucial driver for successful inventory management. With the complexity of supply chains, the advent of e-commerce, and the growing demands of customers, the need for collaboration across various functions and stakeholders has become more evident than ever. In this chapter, we will delve deeper into the importance of collaboration in inventory management and explore its various dimensions.

At its core, collaboration in inventory management is about breaking down silos and fostering communication, cooperation, and alignment between different teams and departments. This collaboration is not limited to internal functions such as procurement, logistics, sales, customer service, and finance, but also extends to external partners such as suppliers and distributors. By working together as a collective force, organizations can optimize their inventory levels, reduce costs, and ultimately enhance customer satisfaction.

One of the primary benefits of collaboration in inventory management lies in achieving better demand forecasting and planning. By sharing information and insights across functions, organizations can enhance their understanding of market trends, customer demands, and promotional activities. This collaborative approach enables more accurate forecasting, leading to improved inventory replenishment strategies and reduced occurrences of stockouts or excess inventory. For instance, a close collaboration between the sales and marketing departments can provide valuable input on customer preferences, upcoming promotions, and anticipated product launches, which can guide inventory planning and optimization efforts.

Furthermore, collaboration facilitates effective inventory control and optimization. When cross-functional teams are involved in the decision-making process, organizations can tap into diverse perspectives and expertise. For example, the collaboration between procurement and operations teams can result in better supplier relationships, improved order processing efficiency, and reduced lead times. By pooling their knowledge and insights, these teams can develop strategies to improve the quality, availability, and cost of supplies, leading to more streamlined and efficient inventory management. Collaboration can also drive the implementation of lean principles and process improvements across functions, helping organizations eliminate wasteful practices and create a more efficient inventory management system.

Collaboration is also instrumental in addressing supply chain disruptions and managing risks. By establishing strong relationships and open lines of communication with suppliers, organizations can ensure a steady and reliable supply of materials or finished goods. Timely collaboration enables swift response to unexpected events such as natural disasters, labor strikes, or shifts in market demand. When various stakeholders, including suppliers and distributors, work together to find alternative solutions or adjust production and distribution plans, the impact of disruptions can be minimized. Additionally, collaboration helps in the identification and management of potential risks, enabling organizations to proactively address issues and safeguard their inventory and supply chain operations.

Moreover, collaboration in inventory management empowers organizations to optimize warehouse operations and layout. By involving warehouse personnel in the inventory planning process, organizations can gain valuable insights into space utilization, storage requirements, and handling efficiency. This collaboration ensures that inventory is strategically located to facilitate efficient order fulfillment and minimize transportation costs. The input from warehouse teams can help identify opportunities for layout improvements, process automation, and inventory tracking technologies, further enhancing inventory management practices.

An often overlooked aspect of collaboration in inventory management is the exchange of data and key performance indicators (KPIs). By sharing data across functions and partners, organizations can gain a comprehensive view of inventory-related metrics such as turnover rates, stock accuracy, and order fulfillment rates. This data-driven collaboration allows organizations to identify areas for improvement, set performance benchmarks, and monitor progress. For instance, through collaboration, organizations can identify trends in demand patterns, seasonality, or SKU performance, enabling them to adjust inventory levels and product assortment accordingly.

Collaboration also plays a pivotal role in ensuring compliance and regulatory adherence in inventory management. By involving legal, compliance, and quality assurance teams throughout the supply chain, organizations can collectively address regulatory requirements, certifications, and standards. This collaborative approach helps organizations mitigate risks related to product quality, safety, and regulatory compliance. For example, by working collaboratively with suppliers and distributors, organizations can ensure that all parties adhere to quality control measures, track batch traceability, and maintain appropriate documentation for audits or inspections.

Lastly, collaboration in inventory management strengthens customer satisfaction and relationships. By sharing information between departments and teams, organizations can gain a holistic understanding of customer preferences, expectations, and demands. This collaborative approach enables organizations to align inventory management practices with customer needs, ensuring timely and reliable product delivery. For example, collaboration between sales and operations teams can facilitate better visibility into customer demand patterns, helping in the development of accurate inventory allocation strategies. By meeting customer demands effectively and consistently, organizations can foster higher levels of customer loyalty and repeat business.

In conclusion, collaboration has transformed from a mere buzzword to an essential enabler of successful inventory management. Its far-reaching benefits encompass better demand forecasting, optimal inventory control, enhanced supply chain resilience, efficient warehouse operations, data-driven decision-making, regulatory compliance, and elevated customer satisfaction. By embracing collaboration as a fundamental principle, organizations can navigate the complexities of modern business and establish a solid foundation for growth and success in their inventory management practices.

The Future of Inventory Management

The Future of Inventory Management:

In recent years, inventory management has undergone significant changes due to advancements in technology and shifts in consumer behavior. As we look ahead, there are several key trends and developments that will shape the future of inventory management.

1. Automation and Robotics: The use of automation and robotics in inventory management is expected to increase significantly. Technologies such as autonomous drones and robots have the potential to revolutionize the way inventory is monitored, counted, and replenished. These technologies can improve efficiency, accuracy, and speed in inventory management processes. For instance, drones can be deployed to conduct automated stock counts in warehouses, eliminating the need for manual scanning or human involvement. Similarly, robots equipped with artificial intelligence (AI) can automatically sort, arrange, and stack inventory items, significantly reducing the time and effort required.

Automation in inventory management can also extend beyond the physical aspects of inventory handling. Robotic process automation (RPA) and machine learning (ML) algorithms can automate routine tasks in inventory management, such as updating stock levels, generating reports, and reconciling inventory data across multiple systems. This not only saves time and reduces errors but also frees up employees to focus on more strategic tasks and decision-making.

2. Internet of Things (IoT): The IoT continues to expand its reach and impact, and it is poised to transform inventory management as well. With the integration of sensors and connectivity, inventory items can be tracked in real-time, providing businesses with better visibility and control over their stock levels. IoT-enabled devices and systems can automate inventory tracking, reduce errors, and facilitate seamless communication between different nodes in the supply chain. For example, smart shelving units fitted with sensors can monitor stock levels and automatically trigger reordering when certain thresholds are met. In addition, smart tags and RFID technology can enable precise and efficient tracking of inventory through the entire supply chain, from manufacturing to retail, reducing loss and

ensuring inventory accuracy.

Moreover, the IoT can enable advanced inventory monitoring and analysis. Data collected from IoT sensors can be analyzed using advanced analytics techniques, such as predictive modeling and machine learning algorithms, to identify patterns and trends in consumer demand, optimize inventory levels, and improve supply chain efficiency. This real-time, data-driven approach can help businesses make proactive decisions, anticipate market shifts, and respond swiftly to changes in customer preferences or demand patterns.

3. Big Data and Analytics: The abundance of data available in today's digital world presents both opportunities and challenges for inventory management. By harnessing the power of big data and analytics, businesses can gain valuable insights into consumer demand patterns, optimize inventory levels, and make data-driven decisions. Predictive analytics can enable more accurate forecasting, reducing stockouts and excess inventory. Moreover, machine learning algorithms can continuously analyze large datasets to identify trends, patterns, and correlations that humans might overlook. This enables businesses to adjust their inventory strategies in real-time, respond rapidly to market fluctuations, and improve supply chain efficiency.

Furthermore, advanced analytics tools can provide actionable insights into inventory performance, such as inventory turnover, carrying costs, and customer behavior. By combining data from various sources, including sales data, market trends, and customer feedback, businesses can gain a holistic understanding of their inventory and make informed decisions about product assortment, pricing, and promotions. This data-driven approach not only improves inventory management but also enhances overall business performance and customer satisfaction.

4. Cloud-Based Inventory Systems: Cloud technology has already transformed various aspects of business operations, and inventory management is no exception. Cloud-based inventory systems provide businesses with flexibility, scalability, and real-time access to inventory data from anywhere. These systems can streamline inventory control processes, improve collaboration between different departments in an organization, and enhance visibility across the supply chain. Moreover, cloud-based inventory systems can integrate with other enterprise resource planning (ERP) software, enabling seamless data exchange and enhancing overall operational efficiency.

Cloud-based inventory systems also offer the advantage of scalability. As businesses grow or expand into new markets, cloud-based systems can easily accommodate changes in inventory volume or complexity without the need for extensive infrastructure investments. Additionally, cloud-based inventory systems provide built-in security features and regular software updates, ensuring the safety and integrity of sensitive inventory data.

5. Artificial Intelligence (AI) and Machine Learning (ML): AI and ML technologies are increasingly being utilized in inventory management to automate routine tasks, analyze complex data sets, and optimize decision-making. AI-powered algorithms can identify patterns, detect anomalies, and suggest optimal reorder points, helping businesses minimize stockouts and reduce holding costs. ML algorithms can also improve demand forecasting accuracy by learning from historical data and adjusting predictions in real-time. Additionally, AI chatbots can assist in inventory queries, providing accurate and quick responses to customers and internal stakeholders.

Another application of AI and ML in inventory management is predictive maintenance. By analyzing real-time data from machinery, sensors, and other systems, AI algorithms can detect potential equipment failures and alert maintenance teams in advance. This proactive approach minimizes downtime, reduces unexpected disruptions in the supply chain, and enhances overall operational efficiency.

6. Omnichannel Inventory Management: With the rise of e-commerce and the growing demand for seamless customer experiences, businesses need to adopt omnichannel inventory management strategies. This involves synchronizing inventory across multiple channels, such as brick-and-mortar stores, online marketplaces, and social media platforms. By integrating their inventory systems and leveraging advanced fulfillment strategies, businesses can provide customers with consistent, on-time deliveries and improve overall customer satisfaction. This may include implementing intelligent order routing systems that consider inventory availability, location, and shipping costs to optimize fulfillment across various channels.

Omnichannel inventory management also requires centralizing inventory data and integrating it with customer data. This enables businesses to have a complete view of their inventory and customer behavior, allowing for personalized promotions, targeted marketing campaigns, and improved demand forecasting. By understanding customer preferences across different channels and aligning inventory accordingly, businesses can optimize stock levels, reduce overstocking or stockouts, and deliver a seamless shopping experience to their customers.

7. Sustainability and Green Initiatives: The future of inventory management will also prioritize sustainability and environmental responsibility. Businesses will need to adopt practices that reduce waste, optimize transportation routes, and minimize carbon footprint. This may involve implementing eco-friendly packaging materials, utilizing renewable energy sources, and partnering with suppliers who adhere to sustainable practices. By incorporating sustainability into their inventory management strategies, businesses can not only reduce their environmental impact but also appeal to socially conscious consumers who prioritize eco-friendly brands.

Additionally, sustainable inventory management practices can lead to cost savings and operational efficiencies. For example, optimizing transportation routes can reduce fuel consumption and greenhouse gas emissions, while implementing reverse logistics processes can enable the recycling or repurposing of products and materials. Moreover, sustainable inventory management can improve brand reputation, attract environmentally conscious customers, and align businesses with industry standards and regulations related to environmental sustainability.

In conclusion, the future of inventory management will be characterized by automation, connectivity, data-driven decision-making, and a focus on sustainability. Businesses that embrace these trends and adapt their inventory management processes accordingly will be better positioned to meet the evolving demands of the market and gain a competitive edge. The integration of technologies such as automation, IoT, AI, and ML will enable businesses to optimize inventory levels, improve supply chain efficiency, enhance customer experiences, and contribute to a more sustainable future. These advancements in inventory management will not only drive operational efficiency but also enable businesses to stay agile and responsive in a dynamic and competitive business landscape.